DEVORAN - A DIFFERENT CORNISH VILLAGE

First published 1990

by

B.J. Simpson
"Narabo Creek"
Devoran, Truro, TR3 6NF

All profits accruing from the publication
of this book will be donated to
Devoran Church for the new Parish Centre

Bibliography:-

I gratefully acknowledge information from the following books:
"A History of Tin Mining and Smelting in Cornwall"1967
"Essays in Cornish Mining History" 1970
"The Redruth and Chasewater Railway 1824-1915"
All by D. Bradford Barton
"The Cornish Miner"
by A.K. Hamilton Jenkin
The Feock and Fal Local History Group books (many out of print)
"A History of Restronguet"
by Dr. W. McC. Graves-Morris
Also "Kelly Directories", the records of the former Devoran
Women's Institute and the Official Censuses of 1841 and 1881

I am also grateful for the assistance of the staffs of the County Record Office, Truro, the Local Studies Department of Redruth Library, Truro Library, Truro Museum, and Messrs. R. Bird, R.S. Acton, W. Trebilcock, R. Ferris, P. George and Miss L. Webber for variously advising, giving interviews and for the use of photographs.

Cover photograph by courtesy of R.N.A.S. Culdrose

Printed by Mid Cornwall Printing, Truro
from the authors origination.

The (Plymouth) "Mary" barge at Devoran towards the end of the industrial maritime era

ISBN 0 9516535 0 4

DEVORAN - A DIFFERENT CORNISH VILLAGE

INTRODUCTION

"As dead as Devoran Docks" the saying went, between the two World Wars, as the creek channels silted up, the workshops decayed, the wharves crumbled at their edges and the gorse took over. The village that had boomed so rapidly a hundred years before, and for a while had become the busiest mining port in Cornwall, had been in decline since 1880. Later on it slowly began to recover as transport links to Truro and Falmouth improved and the presence of basic facilities, Church, school, shops and inn, attracted new building.

I had not lived in Devoran for very long before I became conscious of the uniqueness of my adopted home. Being a keen boat-owner I was fascinated by the various obstructions in the creek and the reasons for the courses of the existing channels. I wondered about the reddish-brown mud that deposited a film on the bottom of my boat within days and which even removed the need for any form of anti-fouling! I knew also that I lived in one of the early buildings of the village and, inspired by local advice as to the previous occupants, I sought out its history in official local sources. It was then that I realised that in the libraries, one could find little books about quite tiny villages, yet no-one had apparently composed one specifically for Devoran which is a village of over a thousand souls and moreover, has as dramatic a history as one could hope to find.

That is not to say that no history has been written of Devoran. Far from it. Its incredibly rich past has prompted several technical books on railways and mining to include chapters on Devoran and its creek. The two local history groups, Feock and Fal, have produced excellent publications that go into matters such as shipbuilding, education, roads and employment in far greater detail than I have. I am indebted to them all for little of my research has been original, consisting as it does of having combed all the sources I could find for items that I felt contributed to a story that was general, rather than detailed, of Devoran and the creek. The result, I hope, gives an account of the formation, prosperity, decline and revival of the popular village of today.

Barry Simpson

Devoran, 1990

THE EARLY HISTORY OF THE AREA

Many towns and villages in Cornwall have been the subject of detailed histories. Their establishment may have been due to their location in relation to the developing industries, usually the proverbial "fish, tin and copper", and many begin around the 13th. - 15th. centuries. At that time, the subject of this book, Devoran, did not exist as a village as such but it warranted an area name to encompass the farms and cottages dotted around the gentle, south-facing slopes to the north of Restronguet Creek. That name "Deffrion", successively became Devrian, Deveron, Devoron then Devoran and derived from the Cornish for "meeting of the trickling waters". Of course, the spelling of place names, and even surnames, wasn't taken too seriously in those days but by about 1840 the name Devoran was quite firmly established.

Writing in the magazine of the Old Cornwall Societies in 1979, Dr. W. McC. Graves-Morris gives the origin of the name Restronguet as Res - a valley; trong - a nose or ness; gas - deep making "A valley with a deep promontory". He says that the prehistoric period knowledge is rather sparse in our area. There are many barrows and burial mounds to be seen, although some have been ploughed in over the years. These relics are thought to be of Bronze Age, around 1,000 years BC. During the subsequent Iron Age there was further immigration of Celtic people from the Continent and they were more advanced than the local "Dumnoni" with whom they merged. Christianity probably came to Cornwall from the Mediterranean by the fifth century AD and was reinforced by missionaries from Ireland, Wales and Brittany. The local tribes adapted peacefully to the Roman administration and, although little is known about the period, Roman coins and a pewter dish have been excavated at Carnon Downs and Devoran. During the Dark Ages, it appears Cornwall was more or less left to its own devices until the tenth century.

The Manor of Restronguet, which included Carclew, gets some mention as early as 1195 and there were several changes in ownership over the next few centuries. Before 1485 the Bodrugans were powerful along South Cornwall from Gorran Haven to Cosawes. Some of their tenants had to send them a pair of white gloves each Michaelmas - unusual , but the fact that the Bodrugan crest contained a white glove no doubt had something to do with it. The Bodrugans other claim to fame, apart from riding a horse over a cliff to escape capture after backing the wrong side against Henry VII, was to face a Court case after a piratical raid on James Trefusis' house on Carrick Roads and on his ship, the "Pride of Feock"!

Carclew was occupied by the Bonithon family for over 300 years after a close shave by the first of the line, who had sided with Henry VII, and had to flee the country until Henry defeated Richard III at Bosworth in 1485. Throughout Cornwall the great families had been on different sides and there were many land confiscations ordered by the Star Chamber before 1500. It was by this means that the Trevanions of Caerhayes came to own most of the land south of the creek for the next 200 years when they sold to the Trefusis family who in turn sold to William Lemon.

The earliest map of the area, by a Portuguese named Boazio, is dated 1597 and has some interesting place names. The curve on the creekside, the eventual site of Devoran, has the name "Penelew Point" - a considerable distance from Penelewey if that was the connection - whilst Point has the more appropriate description of "Tregouse Point", after a nearby farm. Chycoose is also called "Tregouse Cove" whilst Tallacks Creek is shown as "Penelew Cove" although we know that it became "Narabo Creek" by the end of the eighteenth century.

Boazio's map - 1597

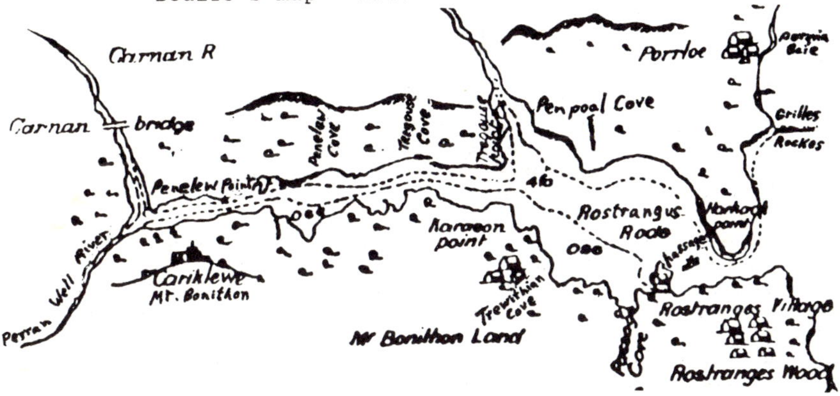

Landowners on the north side of the creek were mainly the Boscawens (Earls of Falmouth) and the Robartes who owned much of the Devoran area from 1577, even before they acquired Lanhydrock in 1620. Over the years the family name changed to Agar-Robartes and the actual owner of the land when building at Devoran was proposed was the Hon. Anna Maria Agar. The Land fronting the creek between Devoran and Restronguet Point was gradually split into smaller units with Lord Falmouth and Sir William Lemon owning most.

As with older centres of population, Devoran's location was its "raison d'etre". The whole of the Carnon Valley including Restronguet Creek (itself a "ria" or drowned river valley) contained large deposits of alluvial tin connected with the main lodes further inland and it cannot be said for certain when man first began to exploit this natural formation. For instance, in 1801 a pick made from deerhorn was discovered in the creek mud and was dated by the British Museum as being between 4,000 and 6,000 years old. Then, in 1823, tinners found a skeleton in a carefully constructed stone grave 22 feet below high water mark in the Carnon Valley. In recording this find, Mr. W. Tregoning Hooper expressed the view that tin mining was taking place here before at least 1,000 BC. The word "mining", applied to this period, does not mean the hard-rock, deep mining that we think of today. Until probably the 17th. century tinning consisted only of either digging for it where it was accessible or streaming for it.

THE BEGINNINGS OF THE INDUSTRIAL REVOLUTION

It was comparatively easy to stream for tin in the upper reaches of the Carnon Valley, which was tidal for some distance above Devoran, and the excavation for it beneath the tens of feet of mud and overburden between tides doubtless began well above Bissoe. As work continued down stream and the incoming tide became more of a problem, it was necessary to build dams to protect the operations and, in 1785, the "Carnon Stream Works" established a vast area where streaming could take place. This was inside banks constructed on either side of Restronguet Creek and these stretched from near the road bridge - not todays bridge but one built in 1754 connecting Carnon Downs with Perran Well - down almost to Chycoose, a distance of about a mile and a half. Without the benefit of mechanised earth-moving equipment this must have been quite an accomplishment.

The two rivers, Carnon and Perran, were diverted to run close to the shores on either side so that navigation was preserved by so-called "tide canals" both to Perranarworthal, where the Fox family were to establish a large and prestigious foundry in 1791, and to Devoran where a small wharf was operating commercially and where some of the houses were occupied by merchants instead of farm workers. Even Mellingey Creek, today just a marsh fed by the Trewedna Stream, was accessible via the channel (seen under today's road bridge on the southern side) leading to a couple of wharves, one of which served the Basset Foundry and which became Visick's works over a hundred years later. It was probably during these mammoth excavations that the deerhorn pick came to light.

In 1778 a mining journal called "Pryces Mineralogies" said that "a Mr. Reed has set up furnaces on Restronguet River for the extraction of antimony" and, although it is not certain where these were sited, it must surely be the same Mr. Reed referred to in 1794 by Alfred Jenkin, the steward of the Agar-Robartes estate, when he reported the potential value of the deep water at Devoran where "Reed has a considerable trade in coals and timber" and recommended further land acquisition. It could well be that these two gentlemen were the founding fathers of Devoran at a time when the tin streaming operation was still at its height. The days of that industry were obviously numbered and, with the growing use of steamships, Jenkin had the foresight to spot possible use of the deeper water left by the opencast mining. There seem to have been several small furnaces established on the banks of the Carnon River towards Bissoe and, before arsenic was found to have commercial value, the noxious fumes were burnt off to the detriment of local residents and the crops in their gardens. More than one legal action resulted from this activity. In years to come, of course, Bissoe was to become a nationally important source of arsenic production.

Sir William Lemon of Carclew had been the major backer of the streamworks and one of the reasons for making the great effort involved in getting at the tin lying about 22 feet down was the declining price of copper whilst tin was more valuable and still in demand. Unfortunately this swing towards tin created a surplus and drove its price down too. Life was incredibly hard and there are stories of women collecting snails for soup and of petitions, followed by near riots, by the men, against the low wages. The "Gentlemans Magazine" in 1789 reported that a protest by tinners near Truro had led to soldiers being called out to subdue it but, although ordered to open fire by the Magistrate, they had refused to do so.

The Perran Foundry went into the production of heavy engineering items in about 1830 and shared a similar fame with Harveys of Hayle on an international basis for many years.

The Perran River, as the channel from the foundry seawards was always known, is fed by the River Kennall which tumbles down through Kennall Vale with such force that its energy was harnessed by a succession of mills by the Kennall Vale Gunpowder Company. Their products were used for blasting in the mines and the Company thrived until the development of high explosives such as dynamite later in the nineteenth century. It continued on some scale however from 1811 until 1910 and afforded some employment to Devoran residents for all of that period.

The Vale today is a Cornwall Trust for Nature Conservation reserve where the remaining industrial ruins, including the many leats, show just how the water was used many times before hurrying down to the foundry for yet further use. It typifies how the once intense use of natural forces can be reclaimed by nature herself over the decades and the almost eerie presence of the relics of the past somehow enhances the sheer beauty and peace that prevail there today.

The industry sounds dangerous and indeed it was. There is a critical moment in the production of gunpowder, when it is being pressed, and the buildings concerned with that stage were built with deliberately fragile roofs so that they could blow off, and be replaced, more easily when an explosion occurred. One recorded incident is of the lady who brought the men their hot pasties from the kitchen and did not see the still red ember clinging to her skirt! Surprisingly, in the 99 years of operation, only seven deaths were reported.

This then was the scene in the early nineteenth century. There were little businesses ancilliary to the mines, factories exploiting the mineral deposits and the water power, barges bringing coals and timber, the foundry at Perran Wharf and the huge open tin stream works. Added to this was the export of copper ore, being laboriously carried to many little waterside places by teams of pack horses over tracks which would become impassable in winter- places such as Weir, Point, Roundwood, Pill, Newham and others on the Fal complex where barges could be loaded.

The Carnon Streamworks closed in 1811, having been said to have made a cumulative profit of £50,000 over its quarter century of operation. A contemporary visitor to the scene described it as "unearthly" with mound upon mound of red mud being carried by men and boys with barrows across planks. There was always the bonus of finding tiny pieces of gold and the streamworkers used to carry goose quills in which to keep the "prills" of gold until they could take them to a goldsmith in Truro. As recently as 1951 an 86 year old resident, a Mr. Edwards, told an interviewer that he recalled his grandfather talking about this.

The second decade of the 19th. century must have been charged with an atmosphere of impending change in Restronguet Creek. It was thought that as much tin as it was possible to stream from the creek had been recovered and unemployment was rife. Indeed, an application from a Mr. Mancur for a mining licence, or sett, in the creek opposite Devoran (County Record Office reference FS 3/1/13-15) drew the following comments from Sir Wm. Lemon in a letter dated 24th. February, 1818, to his agent, Francis Paynter of St. Columb:- "Unwilling as I am to have the river again defaced, and all my comforts at Carclew broken in upon by tinners going all over my grounds, and that for what I am convinced will not answer to the adventurer, yet in these times when everyone is endeavouring to find out labour for the poor, I consider it to be so paramount an object that I cannot think of putting my wishes and comforts in competition with it...... I must not bear the odium of discouraging mining in Cornwall."

This "adventurer" must have intended to work some ground close to the Carclew estate and operating from the "banks" because the letter also refers to the levelling of the banks which Sir William sounded quite pleased about; they must have been a lot higher than they are today. One wonders how successful this man was , and whether it was his results that encouraged the later submarine mining. As for the unemployment, this was only a year before "Peterloo" where, in an up-country confrontation with starving workers, the Riot Act was read and cavalry charged the unarmed protesters. An interesting rental comparison is also recorded in this year - one Peter Swann rented a house, garden and wharf at Devoran for £20 per annum!

The output of the mines in Gwennap, plus their need for coal from S. Wales and the lack of safe harbours on the North Cornish coast, caused those involved to consider using the sheltered creeks on the south coast in spite of the hazardous additional journey around Lands End. This, plus the remaining tin in the creek, no doubt gave rise to the existence of Devoran as we know it today.

CORNWALL.

DEVORON,

NEW TOWN, FLOATING HARBOUR, &c. &c.

PROSPECTUS.

THE Quays at *Point*, *Narabo*, and *Devoron*, in *Restronget Creek*, *Falmouth River*, having been principally occupied by a few Merchants, previous to, and since the completion of the *Redruth Railway*, and the Trade and Commerce thereon having greatly increased, many persons engaged in such Trade have become desirous to obtain independent Wharfs, Quays, and Warehouses.

Specification.—With a view to the accommodation of the Traders in general, and to the establishment of Warehouses, Manufactories, and Works which require Quays, and other such conveniences, a Scite of Land, containing about *Five Acres*, has been selected and set out at *Devoron*, for the erection of Warehouses, Manufactories, &c., and for a Dock or Floating Harbour, situated between the *Rail Road* and the *Channel of the Creek*, which, by the operation of the Sluices and Lock Gates, in receiving the Tidal Stream at high water, and discharging it at low water, will create, and permanently secure, a seaward passage for Vessels of from Two to Three Hundred Tons Burthen, at half tide, and thus form an excellent Port, independent of the casual aid of back water and Land Floods, and thus, also, prevent the necessity of expensive Inland Reservoirs.

The Life of Commerce *(Regularity* and *Dispatch)* can only be sustained by a Port of easy access, by convenient Quays, and by cheap and quick internal communications

These advantages will be found in this favoured situation, in an eminent degree; for, independent of the Vessels being always afloat, the expense of Lighterage will be saved; the Demurrage, Tonnage, and Quayage Labour will be greatly diminished; whilst by the Rail Road and New Turnpike Road, cheap and expeditious Communications are already opened with the principal Towns, populous Villages, and the most wealthy and extensive Mineral District in Cornwall.

The present Trade (consisting of Groceries, Flour, Timber, Coal, Ores, &c.) amounts to *Fifty-five* Thousand Tons annually, with a prospect of increase on the extension of the Rail Road, so considerable as to warrant the estimate of a future Average of, at least, *Sixty* Thousand Tons annually.

The Design for appropriation of this Estate, extends to the erection of a New Town (and the accompanying Plan specifies the Lines of the Roads now making, and the proposed Streets), possessing a Southern Aspect on a gentle Declivity (sheltered on all the other points by an elevated Ridge) commanding the most picturesque Scenery, with beautiful Maritime and Inland Views; a dry Soil and Strata, pure and abundant Springs, excellent Building Stone, and situate adjacent to the Harbour and Communications before described, in a respectable opulent Neighbourhood; but few situations present such advantages for the *Retirement of the Wealthy*, or, for the spirited *Enterprize of Trading* and *Commercial* Men.

SCHEME.

I. The Land for Floating Harbour and adjacent Quays, is offered under the Conditions and Covenants stated in the Speculation, for Fifty Years, at a small Rent for the first Five Years, and a fixed Rent for the remainder of the Term.

II. The Land for Building will be Let also for Fifty Years, at a fixed Rent.

III. The Two principal Roads will be opened from the Turnpike to the proposed Scite for Building by the Lessor, with all possible dispatch.

IV. No Royalty will be required for the Stone from the Quarries, which, previous to the 1st of January, 1834, shall be used upon the Estate; and the Lessees and Tenants will be privileged under the Act in the line of the Rail Road.

V. No Noxious Trades or Manufactories will be permitted upon the Estate.

Information as to Plan, Rents, and all other Particulars, may be had of WILLIAM JAMES, Esq. *Land Agent, Bodmin, and at his Office, Devoron.*

Cornwall County Record Office Reference FS.3/1052

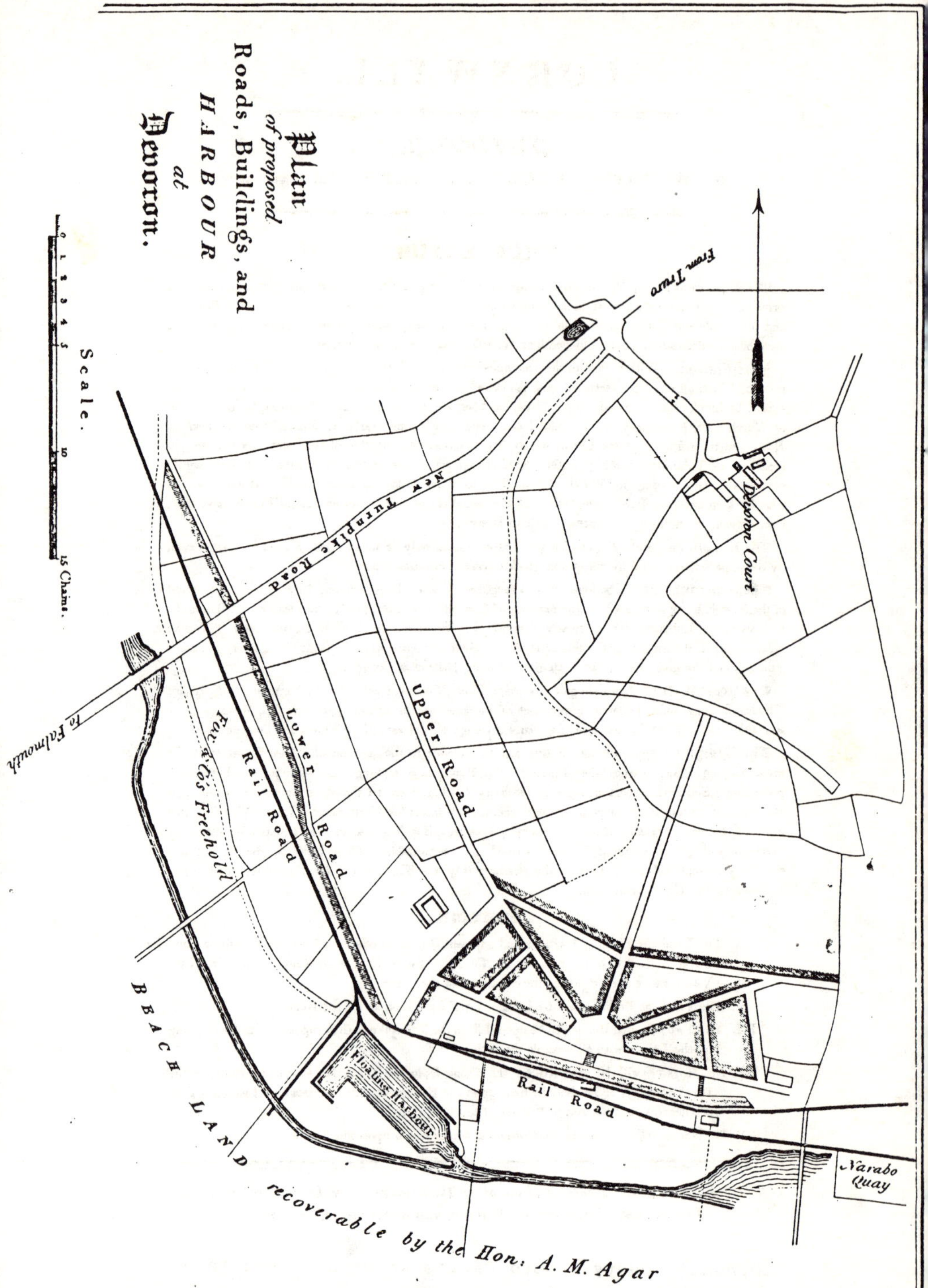

Cornwall County Record Office Reference FS.3/1052

THE RAILWAY, THE DOCKS AND THE GROWTH

It was not long after the closure of the Streamworks that the seaward dam was breached by high tides and gales and this gap was opened up for navigation to what had been the "inside" or mined side of the embankments. Quite quickly a new quay called "Deveron New Quay" was established on the embankment to the east of "Deveron Old Quay" which was on original ground approximately opposite the end of the present Market Street. This can be seen on the map reproduced below which shows not only the proposed site of Narabo Wharf but another wharf close to the old road bridge, to be reached by a new, dredged central channel. Of course, these never came about. Indeed, it was only a few years later that the new bridge (today's A39) was first built.Neither did some of the schemes on the Plan on page 10 materialise. The "floating harbour" never got off the ground and the eventual lay-out of St. Johns, Belmont and Chapel Terraces was different.

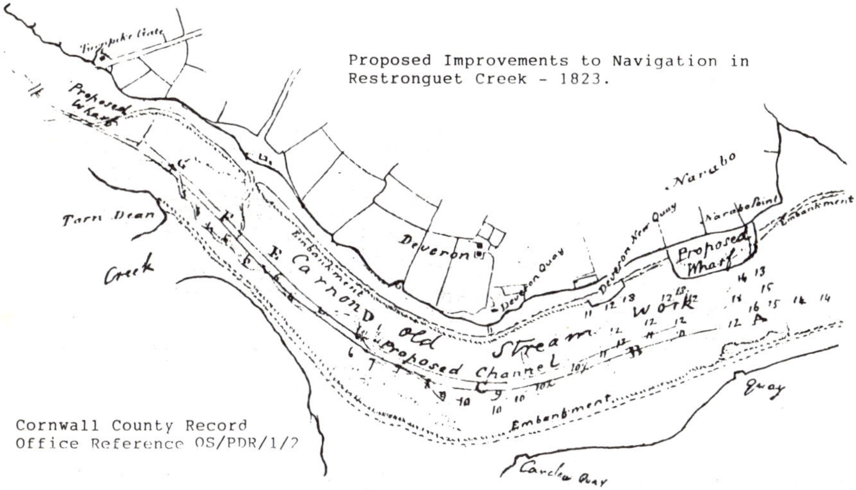

Proposed Improvements to Navigation in Restronguet Creek - 1823.

Cornwall County Record Office Reference OS/PDR/1/2

It appears that the excavations left much deeper water - about 15 feet at high tide - than in the old inshore channel which had only been used by barges while the tin streaming operation was in progress. This channel became moribund and, in 1824, was blocked by the erection of Carnon Stream Mine by Michells of Calenick at what is now known as Carnon Mine, to west of the end of the dam still visible opposite the water pump. This was the start of submarine mining with a pumping engine draining levels some 50 feet below and the same company seem to have constructed other engines on different sites on the Perran or Carclew side of the embankment because of the limited range of the pumping systems.

A plan now at the County Record Office (Ref. M/AD/521) which is too large for reproduction, although a section is shown overleaf, is dated 1832 and gives an excellent "snapshot" of how the early wharves were developed. It shows the three big initial wharves, Fox's, Devoran and Narabo, all using the old embankment as a starting point with the former course of the Carnon River filled in at those points but in others, where timber ponds and quay inlets were needed, the embankment was cut away. Baynard & Companys timber pond was the largest, to the west of Devoran Wharf, and an "island" quay in the middle of the old channel is called "Sambles Wharf". The present Old Quay Inn was referred to as "Messrs. Jennings' premises" and the Railway Offices were at Devoran House. Narabo Quay boasted 12 ore hutches - where stocks were stored by individual owners awaiting shipment - whilst Devoran had 5 plus a cellar and a lime kiln (the wharf was roughly opposite the "Crown & Anchor" now a private house called "Hazeldene"). Fox's Wharf, near the bridge, had 6 hutches and lime kiln. It may be that this plan never intended to show dwelling houses, only the industrial development, but there are certainly very few shown in relation to the two inns which must have anticipated considerable trade from the seafarers and workers.

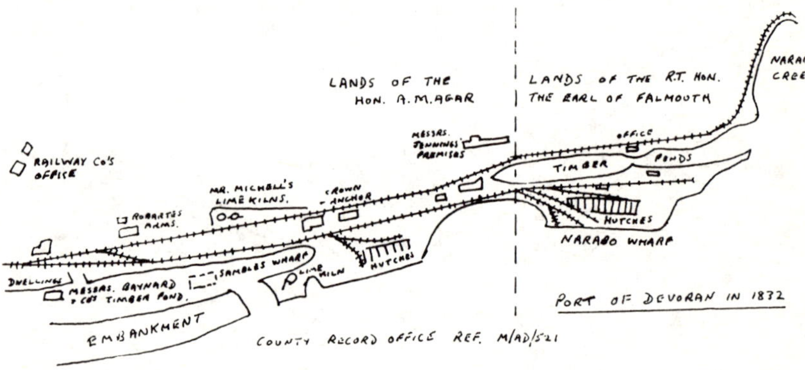

Discussions had previously taken place on likely routes for a mineral railway similar to that which ran to Portreath on the north coast and it was then, in 1820, that another star player in Devoran's future came on the scene. John Taylor was a leading mining entrepreneur and had made a name for himself using the latest methods to re-work older mines. He had just acquired some mines in the Bissoe Valley and he became the main organiser of the scheme to build a 4ft. gauge railway from Redruth to Point which received Royal Assent in 1824. The Redruth and Chasewater Railway as it was known (somewhat misleadingly, as it never served Chacewater) came into being and with it the need for substantial development of Devoran as a village to serve the Railway Company's principal base and the vastly incr-eased trade at the new wharves planned by the Company.

Construction began immediately on the major new wharf at Narabo, just to seaward of Devoran , where the old embankment was made wider and the former Carnon River Tide Canal turned into a timber pond. January 1826 saw the official opening of the Railway, although sections had been in use for several months, and a party of directors and operators travelled the eight miles from Redruth in sixty five minutes. The first wagon carried a banner proclaiming "The first fruits - may the harvest be abundant." After inspecting the Devoran facilities the party were hauled back to Redruth by horse in only one and a half hours.

In 1827 Richard Thomas wrote in his "History of the Town and Harbour of Falmouth" that at Carnon Stream Mine "operations were sufficiently successful to induce the adventurers to extend their works half a mile further down". This was part of their original licence from Sir Wm. Lemon in 1824 for the area from Carclew Quay to Point - he must have had some trouble as anticipated in the earlier licence for on this occasion he stipulated that tinners caught trespassing on the Carclew grounds or woods should be fined £5 and dismissed! Also in 1827 another licence was granted to seaward of the previous one and going as far as Weir. In this instance Lord Falmouth was to receive half of the dues. A year later, by which time the railway was well established, that Company complained that the workings of the Carnon Stream Mine were obstructing navigation and by 1830 the mine had closed, having made a cumulative profit of £28,000 in the six years. In 1832 the Company also took over the Devoran Wharf. Until 1838 Devoran was the busiest mining port in Cornwall for that was before Hayle got its railway but even afterwards Devoran occasionally managed to beat Hayle's figures. The copper ore was brought to the "hutches" on the quays where horses breasted the wagons into position over the appropriate hutch (they were leased by different companies) whereupon the trap doors would be wound open and the contents unloaded. The tin and lead were taken to the smelters at Point in shallower side-opening trucks called "flats" - the others were called "deeps". Road communications had now improved by the opening of the causeway bridge, the present A39.

The present day Old Tram Road, once the additional mile of rail to Point, has a surface that conceals the granite sleepers which carried the rails that were taken up in 1919. From that date until 1951 when it was made up, its condition steadily worsened as the gravel washed away leaving the sleepers protruding. Indeed, people can remember that the footpath across Tallacks Creek was an easier way to walk from Carnon Mine to Devoran - as long as the tide was out! Only horses were used on this section of the line, even after locomotives were in use after 1854. The stables were on Narabo Quay and remains of a chaff-cutter for their feed can still be seen. It would appear that the engines were kept off this Quay. An office to deal with the business of Narabo Quay was built at the side of the Tram Road (now incorporated into a private home) and was linked to the quay by a bridge across the timber pond. It is said that residents of cottages further along the creek were not allowed to walk on the Tram Road and had to keep to the network of footpaths and bridleways that can be followed today.

Two railway workers with a pony used on"The Tram"in 1908

1835 saw yet another ambitious undertaking to get at the rich tin deposits by the establishment of a pumping engine at Yard, below Penpol Creek. The results must have been good but it became obvious that the engine could not cope with the distance the miners would like, and it was decided to create an artifical island in the middle of the creek some 30/40 yards in diameter. A shaft was then driven through it - by covering the cylinder and loading it with 100 tons of silt to drive it down - and a small rotary engine installed beside it. It was said to be a very conspicuous erection and thousands of tons of spoil were produced , accounting for its present size for it is still visible at low water with a cairn of stones at its centre. This mine's peak year was 1838 when 212 men and boys worked it. By 1842 the tin price had fallen to £64 a ton and the mine closed, having produced 638 tons of black tin in seven years. It was reported that tin in quantity and quality was still there.

An official population census took place in 1841 and can be inspected on microfilm at Truro Library. An incomplete section is reproduced overleaf to give an idea of the location and occupations of villagers at that time and to give readers with long local associations an opportunity to check on their ancestors! The records are hand-written and may contain errors in spelling. The area called "Nonesuch" refers to a farmhouse, now no longer in existence, higher up the valley where a stream runs into Tallacks Creek and it is interesting that a member of that family is shown as occupier because at that time the creek was still called Narabo Creek and only changed as the Tallack family rented land by the creekside, later becoming established as smallholders and barge-owners. Certainly they were one of the families to prosper soon after the coming of the railway.

Higher Devoran
Wm. Williams (carpenter)
Edward Pinno
Elizabeth Woolcock
Devoran
Jas. Whitburne (agent)
John Willington (porter)
Hugh Maunder (porter)
Richard Sampson (agent)
Thos. Michell (innkeeper)
John Gilson (smith)
Wm. Tremayne (agent)
Maryann Bishop
Joseph Curtis (sailor)
James Rukin (innkeeper)
Thos. Harris (blacksmith)
Wm. Whitford (miller)
James Wesley (tin miner)
Richard Treweek (broker)
Thos. Killow (tin miner)
Elizabeth Wadon (grocer)
Philip Michell (pilot)
Harry Francis (agent)
Wm. Jane (coal merchant)
Mary Whitburne (milliner)
Robert Sampson (tin miner)
Jacob Welch (butcher)
Henry Bishop (tin miner)
Thos. Trevenna (tin miner)
Mary Francis (grocer)
John Francis (labourer)
Nonesuch
Thomas Tallack (waterman)

Middle Devoran
Thos. Martin (farmer)
Joseph Carveth (waggon driver)
Edward Tregaskis (farmer)
Wm. Daniel (labourer)
Catherine Treweek (grocer)
Richard Coad (farmer)
Elizabeth Scoble
Thos. Mannel
Harriet Edes
Narabo
John Tallack (waterman)
Nicholas Tallack (waterman)
Harriet Woolcock
Weighbridge
Henry Williams (agent)
Richard Williams (copper miner)
Thos. Williams (copper miner)
Henry Williams (copper miner)
Carnon Gate
Nicholas Leverton (lime burner)
Wm. Stephens (carpenter)
Richard Stephens (seaman)
Nicholas Stephens (seaman)
Wm. Stephens (shipwright)
Wm. Wilton (seaman)
Emmanuel Curtis (coal merchant)
Emma Eyres (dressmaker)
Emma Nicholls (innkeeper)
Edward Nicholls (miner)
John Robins (labourer)
John Evans (tin miner)
Edmund Buzza (tin miner)

Devoran School was opened in 1846 as a Church School (actually being used for services by Feock Church whilst Devoran lacked one), becoming a National School in 1863 until 1893 when Local Education Committees were formed. It was extended in 1871 and by 1880 there were 162 pupils. At that time it was the custom for the children to bow to the teacher on entering and leaving the room! Some notable headmasters were Mr. Walker (from 1866), Mr. Daniell (1879 - 1893) and Mr. Cock (from 1893).

The Port of Devoran continued to thrive although silting had become a problem and some dredging was carried out in conjunction with a re-alignment of the Carnon River (which was bringing so much mining spoil down from the County Adit which drained many mines in the Gwennap area). The railway Company invested in a second-hand steam tug, the "Sydney", and in 1854 acquired two steam locomotives to replace the horses on all but the extension line to Point. The engines were "Miner" and "Smelter" and they were joined by a third, "Spitfire" in 1859. A year earlier the "Sydney" had been replaced by a more powerful tug, "Pendennis", which was fitted with mud rakes to churn up the creek bottom on the ebb tide.

In some conditions following heavy silting, larger vessels had to anchor in the pool opposite the Pandora Inn for some of the cargo to be unloaded into barges which were then towed or poled up the creek to their destinations. This entrance of Restronguet Creek had been used commercially for many years. A map of 1823 shows a coal yard on the quay there and it is said that cattle were made to swim across on their way to Truro market. The quay on the Truro side being marked "Market Quay" on that map.

During 1855/6 Devoran Church was built to the designs of J.L. Pearson, the architect later responsible for Truro Cathedral, and dedicated to St. John and St. Petroc. Much building was done in Devoran around this time and, although business tended to ebb and flow with the fluctuating metal prices, it was really the most prosperous time for the village, with new investment still being made prior to the slump which no one then expected. Devoran Methodist Church was built in 1861 and a year later the Carclew estate passed to a nephew of Sir Charles Lemon, Arthur Tremayne. In 1863 the railway Company suffered a setback by the accidental fire which destroyed an engine shed and a coke store. 1868 saw the construction of the sluice pond near the road bridge. This had been suggested before but inexpensive options had proved inefficient. It is there today for all to see, silted up certainly, but complete with its substantially built lock gates which would have been opened on a flood tide to fill the pond then closed until the tide had receded to leave the channel almost dry, whereupon the gates would be opened for the pond's contents to career down the channel scouring out the mud left by each successive tide. The silt thus removed must have settled in Carrick Roads, probably as far as the North Bank below Mylor.

"Miner" pictured in her later years

Lemon Street - now Market Street

The steamship "Erimus" passing Carnon Mine

Unfortunately for the entrepreneurs, 1870 brought a recession in the mining industry. Lower copper prices caused many mining families to emigrate from such places as Carharrack, St. Day and Lanner, amongst many others, to Australia, America and South Africa. Nevertheless, tin prices were still good and the then manager of the Redruth & Chasewater Railway, Charles Dyke Taylor, had been investigating the possibility of a tin mining operation in the creek in order to exploit what was thought to be a previously unworked area between Carnon Stream Mine and Carnon Yard Mine. In 1871 a sett was obtained from the Tremayne family by the Taylors and a Thomas Woolcock.

A shaft was sunk on the shore at Point which was very deep and from it a horizontal tunnel went out to a ventilation shaft in the creek. The remains of this, "Charles' Shaft", can be seen today and it had been sunk by positioning a loaded barge over each section of cylinder at high tide and leaving the ebb tide to allow the barge to settle down pushing the sections lower into the mud every day. A network of levels were extended under the creek and, in 1872, contact was made with the old workings of Carnon Stream Mine which were said to be in very good order. In 1873, its peak year, the mine employed 67 men and boys but tin prices began to fall and Taylor tried to sell the mine as a going concern in 1874 without success. Mining ceased and Taylor himself died in 1876, aged only around 30. In 1879 the mining equipment was auctioned off. This period was really the beginning of the end for industry in Devoran. The winter after Taylor's death brought severe gales and rainstorms which, with exceptionally high tides, caused a great deal of silt to wash over the "training bank" intended to keep the shipping channel clear of the substances brought down by the Carnon River and it was said that navigation was never the same again. In 1879 the railway Company was put into Receivership, bankrupt in effect but continuing operation under the Receiver's direction.

The Church must have been prospering because Devoran became an Ecclesiastical Parish independent of Feock in 1873. A very good Ordnance Survey map was produced in 1880, shown overleaf, and showing accurately the buildings then in existence in Devoran. At that time the population was about 1200. The Railway Superintendent was James Williams and his clerk was F.J. Tyacke who later became the last manager. Nine Master Mariners lived in the village and the pilot was Thos. Michell. Nicholas Tallack was not only farming but also acting as School Attendance Officer and Rate Collector. The school was run by Mr. R.J. Daniell with Miss Laura Webber as assistant. Lord Robartes was "Lord of the Manor" and sponsor of the Church living, then worth £160 p.a. Mr. Lobb of Carnon Gate was described as a "medical botanist". One of the principal traders were Messrs. Vivian & Co., mainly in coal, and in earlier years their ships "Morfa" and "Augusta" made two trips a week to Swansea and back but, by the 80's, the main shipowners were a Falmouth Company running the "Erimus" and the "Trefusis". John Sims, born in 1861, spoke in 1943 of remembering some other steamships - "Ogmore", "Effie", "Bains", "Netherton" and "John Brogdon". He saw the "Pendennis" towing four barges at a time and other tugs (presumably Falmouth based) "Effort", "Lioness" and "North Star". He also recalled a vitriol works by the old bridge and a timber yard by the sluice pond.

Jewel Villa
Rose Cottage
Reservoir
Middle Devoran
Quarry
Vicarage
Grave Yard
St John's Church
Market House
Belmont
Narabo
Devoran
Methodist Chapel
Park View
Commercial Inn
Engine House
Wharf
Coal S
Lime
Smithy
Talla
Cree
C.C.L.W.
Tides
MYLOR Pᴴ
LXIV.15
KERRIER Hᴰ
76
77
1880

One of the lesser known, and very unpleasant, trades that grew up ancilliary to the mines was the "ochre works" of Messrs. Beer, Musgrave & Co. at Bissoe. This made use of the "Great County Adit", a huge tunnel that drained many mines in the Gwennap district and which emerged at Bissoe to feed into the Carnon River. Workers had to wade up the adit when conditions permitted to collect the ochre which, after treatment at the works, was used for painting the walls of cottages.

The early issues of the Devoran Parish Magazine - begun by the then curate, the Rev. Jellicoe - cover mainly Church business, as now, but little glimpses emerge about the social life of the village at that time. It had a circulation of about 80 and was sold, for 1½d., by Tobias Mitchell in Devoran and by Mrs. Bath at Point.

January, 1889 - In publishing the rules for the Sunday School, meticulous details were given for the award of "good conduct" and "attendance" marks and for the disallowance of marks by the teacher (minor faults such as the loss of one mark for leaving one's Prayer Book at home) or by the Superintendent. Persistent bad behaviour in either Sunday School or Church would be referred to him and he had the power to give a "bad mark" which was equal to the loss of six ordinary marks. On the "carrot" side of the equation, there was the summer treat and the chance of a prize at Christmas but these were strictly conditional on sufficient attendance and ability at saying lessons.

February, 1889 - "We are sorry to have to report that our Church Bell is cracked. This fact has been apparent to all who have heard its sounds for the last fortnight. For some time the bell has received rough usage, and in total ignorance of this, permission was given to ring the bell on New Year's Eve, when the mischief was done". - perhaps the damage was due to the quality of the celebration!

July, 1892 - National School Report - "....now that education is free to the parents, the Managers earnestly hope that they will do their very best to send their children with regularity, although they fear that there are some who with free education do not appear to value the punctual attendance of their children as they did when they paid for their education."

July, 1892 - "We think the teachers of our Sunday School might regularly mark their registers and encourage the scholars to be more regular, and even might find out from their homes the cause of absence, and use their influence with the parents".

October, 1892 - "Three bracket lamps have been fixed upon the walls of the Church with vulcan burners, as it is thought more light is needed".

Striking among regular features were the far higher mortality rates in the young and middle age groups, the prominence of Temperance Societies (even for children from 8 years upwards) and the magic lantern shows or musical evenings for entertainment. Cookery recipes were given and these featured plain, rather stodgy, dishes requiring cheap and readily available ingredients.

The then Vicar was a cricket enthusiast so there were reports of matches; one regular fixture was against the boys training ship H.M.S. Ganges at Mylor which had a reputation for spartan if not cruel conditions.

For some of the treats the children walked to Perranwell Station for the train, and walked back in the evening. The Hon. John and Lady Margaret Boscawen, who lived at Tregye, were great supporters of the Sunday School events.

An Edwardian picnic on the "banks"

Although the docks and the railway were on the wane now, business continued and Devoran seemed quite prosperous. It is reported that the landlady of the Commercial Inn (now the Old Quay Inn) went up to bed on a Saturday night with her apron doubled up with sovereigns and half sovereigns!

1881 saw another National Census and this shows, apart from more people than in the 1841 list, a greater variety of trades. Often, where the head of the house had a certain trade, his sons would take the same one, as apprentices or his assistants. St. Johns Terrace was THE place to live as most occupiers there had a general domestic servant, usually a girl as young even as twelve. Houses in Belmont and Chapel Terraces seem to have been rather over-crowded on the night of the census, many with lodging sailors. Again, the list is reproduced and some local readers will see grandparents or great grandparents in it. Some names have disappeared. Some are remembered for their skill - Hugh Stephens the shipbuilder, the Taylors who brought the industry. The Tallacks gave their name to a creek! Probably the most common name was Michell, with or without a "t", and there are many others who still have local associations or have not moved far away.

Carnon Mine
Hugh Rowe (Master Mariner)
Thomas Rowe (Mariner)
Edwin Rowe (Sailmaker)
John Francis (Miner)
Thos. Pope (Coal porter)
Wm. Pope (Mason)
Hugh Stephens (Shipwright)
John Gay (Mariner)

Narabo
Thos. Paull (Locomotive driver)
Wm. Mitchell (Coal weigher)
John. Willington (Farmer)
Nich. Tallack (Asst. overseer)
Thos. Mitchell (Copper prcptr.)
Wm. Daniell
Thos. Tregaskis (Horse driver)
Thos. Tregaskis (Ship carpenter)

Devoran
George Harris (Plumber)
Jas. Williams (Mine surveyor)
Cath. Moyle (Domestic servant)
James Gillam (Vicar)
George Taylor (Railway Manager)
Eliz. Bovey (Housekeeper)
Thos. Chegwidden (Gardener)
Thos. Williams (Ships stoker)
James James (Labourer)
Hy. Richards (Retd. Mine agent)
Cath. Burrows (Domestic servt.)
John Dowrick (Retd. carpenter)
Eliz. Lobb (takes boarders)
Wm. Mitchell (Master Mariner
Edwin Lidgey (Clerk)
Rebecca Chynoweth (servant)
John Banfield (Master Mariner)
Wm. Johns (Postal messenger)
George Vincent (Engine fitter)
Robt. Whitburn (Rtd. mariner)
Rich. Mitchell (Shipping agent)
Maria Kingsman (Dom. servant)
Edith Keast (" ")
Eliz. Snell (" ")
Wm. Lidgey (Coal merchant)
Wm. McAdams (Customs Officer)
Wm. Nettle (Rtd. silver miner)
Thos. Woolcock (Grocer/draper)
Emily Yeoman (Schoolmistress)
Wm. Carter (Mariner - unemp.)
Wm. Peters (Sailmaker)
Jas. Pengelly (Rtd. coalporter)
Rich. Tippett (Bargeman)
Thos. Michell (Pilot)
Jno. Webber (Railway carpenter)
Walter Webber (" platelayer)

Devoran (contd.)
John Clark (Shipowner)
Rich. Clark (Master Mariner)
Eliz. Mitchell (Rtd. Innkeeper)
Rich. Tyack (Shoemaker)
Eliz. Sprague (Dom. servant)
James Salter (Accountant)
Wm. Hodge (Master Mariner - unemployed)
John Solomon (Farm labourer)
John Husson (Ropemaker)
Eliz. Farquharson (Private school mistress)
Eliz. Sampson (Income from land)
John Sampson (Clerk)
(their house had a housemaid, cook and parlourmaid)
John Phillips (Lime burner)
George Adams (Mariner)
Sarah Bowen (Milliner)
Frdk. Strike (Shipwright)
Chas. Nicholls (Waterman)
Wm. Nicholls (Bargeman)
Janie Nicholls (Pupil teacher)
Wm. Clear (Railway guard)
Solomon Martin (Carrier)
Hannah Martin (Dressmaker)
Susan Warren (Private school)
Herbert Peters (Mariner)
Wm. Mitchell (Blacksmith)
Hannibal Mitchell (Smiths striker)
Wm. Vine (Butler - unemployed)
George Lloyd (Sailor)
Hy. Andrewartha (Engine fitter)
Wm. Dunstan (Carpenter)
George Prinn (Tin smelter)
Phil. Mitchell (Asst. Harbourmstr.)
Wm. Opie (Sailor)
Emmanuel Curtis (Carrier)
Eliz. Trenerry (Dom. servant)
Peter Collins (Grocer)
John Gribble (Ironmonger)
Annie Bray (Pork dealer)
Jas. Rickard (Police officer)
Hy. Opie (Bargeman)
Cath. Pascoe (Chapel keeper)
Samuel Pascoe (Postmaster)

Carnon Gate
Thos. Lobb (Farmer)
George Dana (Sailor)
James Jury (Farmer)
Phil. Docking (Railway watchman)
Ed. Nicholls (Woodsmans labourer)
Wm. Bishop (Butcher)
Robt. Woodranger)

The sailing barge "Mary" and the steamer "Erimus" at Devoran Quay

A prosperous-looking resident pictured in St. John's Terrace

The village appears to have housed two inventors; George Burrell, shown as licensee of the "Crown & Anchor" in 1875, and a Mr. Hewitson, said to have invented the spring interior mattress but to have spent too much developing less successful ideas and to have died in poverty. William Murdoch is reputed to have carried out some early experiments in coal gas lighting at Devoran.

By 1893 Miss Sarah Pascoe had taken over as postmistress from her father Samuel and the village constable was Mark Bennett. There were now only seven master mariners and Joseph Michell was the pilot.

One of the quirks of the progress of Devoran appears to be that, although the commercial success accelerated rapidly after the building of the railway, the development of the residential part of the village was quite slow. The initial plans of the Agar-Robartes Estate did not achieve their fruition until the building, say, of St. Johns Terrace in the 1850s and yet by 1880 the railway was in receivership and the decline had begun!

The early 1880s also saw the demise of the foundry at Perran but the revival of the former Basset Foundry on the banks of the Trewedna Stream by Walter Visick was to become important to Devoran for the next three quarters of a century. Visicks became known as resourceful general engineers and provided a welcome boost for local employment. Perran Foundry became a corn and grist mill run by the Edwards family from 1890 to 1934.

Tops'l schooners at Devoran at low tide

Three steamships alongside Narabo or Lower Quay

Market Street around the turn of the century

Miner at work during the closing years of the railway
(photo by R.T. Courtis)

Railway repair shop workers pictured in 1910

One of the last mining ventures in the creek was authorised in 1907 when Capt. W.F. Tremayne granted a licence to William Coppin Wicket of Redruth (County Record Office ref. WH 2006). The area was quite large, even down to Harcourt (or Harkett as was sometimes called). There appears little evidence of the success or otherwise of this effort; certainly if it had been a major scheme then more would have been recorded. It was probably a "re-working" operation.

In 1914 the master mariners were down to only two, although the pilot was still available. The population had fallen by two hundred and a year later the railway closed. The last large trading vessel, an auxiliary schooner left in 1916 although the barges, chiefly bringing limestone, continued to use the quays. Much of the railways rolling stock was said to have been commandeered during the War, which must have been a cheerless period for the village.

An excursion steamer about to leave Devoran - July 1907

BETWEEN THE WARS - SLOW RECOVERY

1919 records show that the school was now under Truro and Falmouth Education Committee. Mr. W.R. Cock was still the headmaster assisted by the Misses Rowe, Quick and Martin. We are now in the realms of living memory and pupils of the school at this time remember the "copper-plate" handwriting that was insisted upon and consider that the school was very efficient. The principal landowners were shown as Capt. Tremayne, Lord Falmouth and Lady Margaret Boscawen.

In this year Devoran Women's Institute was formed, one of the earliest in Cornwall, and their records have been the source of much interesting information from then on. Also in 1919, Lord Clifden gave the "Park" as a War Memorial and a permanent open space and playground. It is invaluable to the School for sports.

Industry was gradually being wound up after the closure of the railway and docks and the Penpoll Smelting Company finally closed in 1921. In addition to tin smelting, lead had also been dealt with at Penpoll and a huge square chimney once dominated the area (see photo below). It also appeared in contemporary prints and in an interesting watercolour now in Truro Museum. One record states that the lead came from Perranzabuloe and from near Newlyn, although this may have meant St. Newlyn East.

Looking towards Point from Carnon Yard, 1910

1922 saw the introduction of a daily motor bus service to Truro and Falmouth. Prior to this there had been a twice weekly horse bus service operated by a Mr. Dungey whose daughter had married Tom Lavin, a railway worker who featured in several early 20th century photographs and who contributed his memories to writers well into the 70s. He had worked for the Redruth & Chasewater Railway until its closure.

In 1923 Mr. R.M. Sampson, whose family had played a managerial role in the village for many years and who had previously lived at "Killigarth", gave the brass lectern to the Church in memory of his children.

The population hovered around the 1,000 mark in the twenties and thirties. Mr. Cock still ran the School and Joseph Michell was listed as Pilot up until 1930, although Master Mariners had ceased to appear in the street directory. The W.I. archives record the slow march of "civilisation" - in 1928 they asked Truro R.D.C. for a refuse collection to replace the village "dump" at the head of a silted-up timber pond. 1930 saw the installation of electricity in the Village Hall, formerly a railway repair shop, and in that year also the first Devoran Spring Flower Show was held, an annual highlight to this day. In 1931 the weekly "scavenger cart" requested earlier began operation and the Devoran Players gave two performances of "Lord Richard in the Pantry" of which a local critic made the observation that "professional companies have put on far less entertaining shows".

Lord Falmouth's family sold the freehold of Narabo Quay, 21 acres in all, including a little cottage on the Tram Road that had originally served as an office. Messrs. Vivian's quay and office continued operating, mainly as coal merchants. There were still at least eight shops, including a shoemaker and a draper. Their prosperity is a matter for conjecture but, even with a daily bus service, most villagers would have used their local shops as the number of car owners could probably have been counted on one hand.

Some traders in the 1930s and earlier included:- Mrs. Jane Dixon (grocer), Mrs. Susan Currow (draper), Miss Meta Michell (grocer - as a child she did well both at school and Sunday school and later became a pupil teacher), Mr. H.H. Moor, Miss Nora Roberts (grocer), Mr. J.M. Skewes (cobbler), Mr. Harry Solomon (Post Office & stationer), Mr. Harry Sweet (cobbler) and Mr. William Bray who made special leather sea boots for the men who worked on the barges. Mr. James Martin's baker's shop at the bottom of Market Street delivered bread around the village by horse-drawn van. Children were often sent to fetch milk, butter, eggs and cream from local farms, sometimes rowing across the creek for them.

On the 5th. April, 1934 Carclew House, former home of the Lemons and the Tremaynes, was destroyed by fire. It was never rebuilt and today its ivy-covered remains stand gaunt and fenced off for safety. The lands of the old Manors of Carclew and Restronguet were divided and sold.

In 1939, when war loomed, the Parish (Feock Civil Parish) was told that it would be expected to find homes for 268 evacuee children should hostilities break out. Later on, the local Agricultural Production Committee organised the felling of the beech woods in the Carclew grounds as the need for home-produced food grew (the U boat blockade was sinking many ships bound for Britain and imports were mainly those needed for the war effort).

The largest local industrial contribution must have been made by Visicks, the engineers, who had boomed in the 1914-18 war but had experienced mixed fortunes between the wars. They had tried their hand in many markets, cooking ranges, grates, etc. during the housing boom but had found more success with goods needed for drainage and road and water schemes locally. With the advent of mains electricity they turned their skills to various munitions-related jobs, even parts for the "Bailey Bridges" that enabled fast-moving armies to cross major rivers.

FLAG OFFICER IN CHARGE ★ FALMOUTH

Permission is granted to this craft to move at night on ferry & timber rafting duty within Restronguet Creek i.e. North of the Restronguet Bar ferry line.

B Crossley Meates

Lt. R.N.V.R.
21. 3. 44.

BOAT PERMIT

DUTY CLAUSE A.

Office of Flag Officer-in-Charge,
Falmouth Area.

Date 8. 7. 42.

No. F. 1939.

Permission is hereby given for Mr. A. C. George.

Address Point, Devoran, Truro, owner of JO JO
TO HOLD this craft in the area DODMAN POINT westabout to HARTLAND POINT including SCILLY ISLANDS.

Provided the person in charge carries its numbered card this craft may be used subject to current restrictions and in accordance with Admiralty Orders.

1. No movement is to take place between sunset and sunrise or in the thick weather, save with the permission of the local Naval Authority.
2. UNDER DUTY CLAUSE D the Seaward limit of movement is the mouths of the Estuaries in this area except with special Route-pass obtained by personal application at a Naval Base.

   UNDER DUTY CLAUSES A, B, C and E movement as requisite for duty.

   SCILLY ISLES AREA.—Between sunrise and sunset within 2 miles of the Islands and only to the East of the Longitude of Bishops Rock Lighthouse.
3. **ANCHORING, TRAWLING AND GROUND FISHING IS PROHIBITED WITHIN** ONE CABLE OF OBSTRUCTIONS AND/OR the following areas:—

   HELFORD. A Helford area bounded—**On the East** by a line between Mawnan Church and Nare Point. **On the West** by a line between Porth Saxon or Cows Beach and Bosahan Boat House.

   PADSTOW. Also a Padstow area—from a line joining the Coastguard Station and Trebatherick Point to a line joining Padstow Harbour and Rock.

   Skippers of Craft who fish or move outside the permitted areas, disregarding the instructions by the competent Authorities, will be liable to severe penalties and to be fired on.
4. Each craft whether in use or not requires a separate permit sheet.
5. The name should be marked legibly on all craft. The number and letter of the permit is to be clearly painted on each side of the bow, and maintained legible at 50 yards.
6. The Ships and Aircraft (Transfer Restriction) Act 1939 forbids the sale transfer of Ship or mortgage on any British Ship the propulsion of which is in advance of oars, except with the sanction of the Minister of War Transport obtainable per H.M. Customs Offices. All such transactions in the above area require the re-issue of this Naval permit.
7. This permit is not an authority for the supply of fuels. Any craft other than a registered Fishing or Public Ferry Boat seen motoring afloat will be reported to the Police by H.M. Patrols.

   The card issued with this permit is not valid unless signed in ink by the Owner. It is to be held by the person in charge ready at all times for inspection by any Naval, Military or Police Authority.
8. Craft may not go alongside vessels in harbour, or within 100 yards of Falmouth Docks, without special permission endorsed on Naval Permit card, and they are to keep clear of convoy craft. They approach Minesweepers at their peril.
9. Wireless and Radio Transmitters may not be carried.
10. Cameras and sketching forbidden. Plying for pleasure is prohibited.
11. All craft when unattended are to be immobilised in accordance with Admiralty Regulations. They may be padlocked to their moorings.
12. Amendments to these restrictions may be posted on the official notice boards of coastal Police Stations and Customs Offices from time to time. You are obliged to keep yourself informed. Any contravention of the regulations will be summarily dealt with under the Defence (General) Regulations, 1939.

MINES MAY EXIST IN ALL AREAS THE ADMIRALTY DISCLAIMS ALL RESPONSIBILITY

B Crossley Meates

Devoran and Carnon Downs Platoon of the Home Guard

Back Row: Frank Dymond, Reg Crocker, Walter Hoar, Ron Barley, Doug Connor, Lax Collins, Gerald Lean, Albert Opie, Harry Crocker.

Second Row: Jimmy Ferris, Tom Sleeman, Ken Hoare, ? Albert Green, Ernie Pengelly, Bill Gay, Alfie Johnson, Percy Jeffery, Stan Ford, Walter Collis, Arthur Tregaskis, Percy Nicholls, - Truan, Sid Rosevear, Jack Connor, Bill Marshall, Charlie Rosevear, ? .

Seated: Reg Michell, Bunny Dunstan, Harry Davey, George Knight, Harry Solomon, - Teague, Percy Hawke, - Evans, Alec Grey.

Kneeling: Alfie Williams, Henry Woolcock, Fred Knuckey, Clarence Burrows, Tom Hitchens, Gordon Clift, Charlie Bryant, Joe Carlyon, Arthur George, Bernard Pooley, ? , Tom Barker.

The Devoran platoon of the Home Guard was based at the former tollhouse near the road bridge and had been organised by local old soldiers who had survived the first World War when no less than 17 Devoran men were killed on war service. The 1939-45 war claimed fewer lives, eight, and both lists appear on a War Memorial in Devoran churchyard.

The ruins of Carclew House

1945 - PEACE AND PROGRESS

The immediate post-war years saw some efforts to re-start the Devoran Regatta but they did not achieve continuity. Possibly by then the depth of water had diminished and the larger boats could no longer come up that far. In 1950 the Old Tram Road hit the news as the County Council proposed to adopt and tarmac it, at a cost of £2,768, levying a charge on the frontagers. The latter immediately disclaimed responsibility on the grounds that it was a railway, not a road (the 1824 Act had not been repealed). It was a nice try but the processes of law meant that, in the end, they had to pay up and look cheerful! From then on the Tram Road, for all its narrowness and tight corners (or possibly because of them!) became a Mecca for walkers, bird watchers, cyclists, horse riders and for folk who just like to wander along enjoying the views of the creek and the wooded slopes on the south shore. Few creeks have such a public path on one side and no development on the opposite bank.

The Festival of Britain in 1951 was designed to drive away the austerity blues (sweets were still rationed until 1953!) and the local Devoran W.I. compiled a commemorative book giving a snapshot of life in the village at that time - it is now in the County W.I. office in Truro together with another produced in 1965. A photograph of the eastern end of Quay Road shows only

"Quay House" on the shoreline and there is an interesting comment on everyday life compared with "the old days" - "most of the men now work at Falmouth Dockyard and come home on the 5.36 bus to a peaceful, quiet atmosphere - what a contrast!" Time flies and in 1951 there were still plenty of villagers able to recall memories of Devoran's industrial heyday:- "Hugh Stephens' shipyard was near the stones leading to the causeway to Point" and "there was an overhead bridge by the Crown and Anchor". The 1965 book refers to Mr. Tyacke, the last manager of the railway, who founded a Boys' Brigade Unit, and to his daughter who began the Devoran Girl Guides. It also mentioned that "the lower road has six new houses this year" and there was a reference to a barge which spent some months in the creek boring for tin samples.

In 1965 too, a local newspaper highlighted the old dock area as an ideal and little-known picnic spot. This did not last long in the case of Quay Road where the filled-in timber ponds and quays became building sites for attractive bungalows with water frontage and peaceful views across the shallow creek so rich in bird life. The remaining area of undeveloped quay - the first to be built by the railway company and the farthest seaward - was purchased by public subscription in 1988 and "conservation" and "preservation" are the new names of the game.In addition to the building of new houses on an "infill" basis in the existing roads, "New Devoran" in the form of two modern developments on the western side of the village and nearer to the A39, were constructed in the 1970s and 1980s.

1973 saw the formation of the Restronguet Creek Society, a residents association for all who live in the environs of the creek. It acts as a watchdog organisation to ensure the protection of the natural amenities of the area as pressure grows with development, both residential and commercial. All planning applications are carefully vetted and responsible and constructive suggestions are often made. The Society has a large membership and enjoys the respect of the local Councils and other bodies.

In 1982 Liverpool University carried out an ecological survey in connection with a proposal by Billaton Minerals to dredge the mud from the creek by electric suction methods in order to extract the remaining tin which the less sophisicated systems of the Victorian miners had left. Local opposition was strong and a fall in the tin price made the project unviable.

In 1984 Devoran Regatta was resumed on what should be a permanent basis and, although the elegant steam launches seen in Edwardian photographs have been replaced by windsurfers, the traditional "punts" and "lug and mizzens" still feature.

After being run by successive members of the family since the last century, Visicks closed in 1986. In the post-war years it had diversified into such different items as small components for the building trade and shipbuilding on a scale compatible with the size of their premises and what road transport could handle. One of their larger contracts had been the Ross Bridge at Penzance. After only a year of idleness, the premises were again being used by an engineering firm but, as I write, there is a doubt about its future. Men, mostly now retired, who had served apprenticeships in the firm were justly proud of their training and the certificates they were awarded had stood them in good stead in getting employment in this country and abroad.

Devoran Regatta - 1910

1987 - "lug and mizzens" still going strong

DEVORAN TODAY

The new houses have brought families and the Primary School thrives, as do the Church, Chapel and many sports, social and youth interests. The Spring Flower Show celebrated its Golden Jubilee in 1990 and the Devoran Players still produce an annual pantomime. Pressures on the area now stem from greater traffic as tourism continues to grow and the demand for housing so near the growth area that Truro has become.

The trade of shipwright today is rather confused as there is so little building of boats in timber and the "finishing work" inside an alloy or fibreglass hull is more akin to carpentry when compared to the skill required in building a boat from the keel upwards. However, in Devoran the craft is perpetuated in truly traditional manner by Ralph Bird who, in his shed at Carnon Mine, is enjoying strong demand for the Pilot Gigs that he builds for local clubs to race. They are constructed from Cornish narrow-leaf elm and the timbers, or ribs, are steamed so as to be flexible enough to be hand-worked into the shape of the designed hull which is around 30ft. long. The amount of publicity generated by this one-man industry is an indication of the rarity of the skill. Ralph is descended from Hugh Stephens whose artistry in shipbuilding is acclaimed in several books on the subject.

Just as I have been able to incorporate memories of earlier residents thanks to interviewers in years gone by, it seems appropriate to record the recollections of some of today's older citizens, especially as they represent the last of a generation who can still remember the industrial period of Devoran's history. The late Reg Michell of Chycoose told me that he remembered fishermen, early this century, calling the creek "Strangwidge Creek" - my first thought was that the beer must have been stronger then but this does tie up with earlier recorded pronunciations which included "Strunget", "Strangway" and "Stranweke". He also recalled that the centre of the three channels, the much-diverted Carnon River, was referred to as the "Mundic channel". This may have been because of the mine waste that the river brought down or because of the composition of the banks that helped separate it from the shipping channels. He had only praise for his former headmaster at Devoran, Mr. Cock, whose tuition had, he thought, set him apart from other village-educated boys when he went on to senior schools. I have been fortunate to be able to talk to Mr. W. Trebilcock, Miss L. Webber and Mr. R. Ferris, who can all remember the trains and the steamers, and I think that their memories of seemingly unimportant items illustrate the huge changes that have occurred in village life in this century - and not all for the better, some would say!

Wm. Trebilcock - born 1899

I was born at Lower Chypit, a name which has disappeared from use today as it has been incorporated into "Chycoose", the little bay near Point, whilst in my youth Chycoose was just the farm a short way inland. I went to live in Narabo Vale when I was four for several years and then to Bleak House, also on the Old Tram Road. Devoran School was run by Mr. Cock and the infants teacher was Miss Quick. Her nickname was "Billie" and her classroom was the one immediately on the right of the main entrance. In the back of the room was a stepped gallery where I sat (and often hid behind the harmonium). This is the only part of the original school building left. Other teachers were Miss Annie Harris and Miss Michell (daughter of Tobias Michell, the grocer on the corner), both natives of Devoran. Once our ball broke the window of Mr. Gribble's ironmongery shop opposite and we all had to pay a halfpenny each towards it.

Smartly dressed Devoran pupils in St. John's Terrace

Ships were still coming up the creek when I was a boy. The "Erimus" and "Trefusis" amongst them, using mainly the Lower Quay but smaller steamers, the "Danesgate" and "Friargate" came right up to the quay near the bridge. The pilots were Joe Michell and John Opie. Sometimes the ships' loads had to be lightened into barges at Restronguet. The ships had to make a tight turn off Chycoose and there was a buoy there that they used to turn on.

I first worked at the carpenters shop at the side of the timber pond at Narabo (no trace of it now). The little shop in the end of the house facing down the Tram Road was run by Mary Michell and she sold everything from sweets to paraffin, doing a big trade with the sailors who bought tobacco which she cut from a roll. Soon I went to work on a sailing barge, the "Mary" which brought up stone from Porthoustock. She had an engine fitted in 1926 which made life much easier and I was on her until 1932. Another barge, also called "Mary", brought limestone from Plymouth to what we called Lime Kiln Quay, opposite the old railway offices in Quay Road. Lime was produced for the building trade.

The coal porters had to work hard. They wheeled it ashore in barrows. There was the Lower Quay gang and the Vivian's Quay gang. There was also a coalyard by Carclew Terrace. The railway company owned a barge that was different from others - it was decked in and had a raised coaming round the hatch. It was used to take tin ingots to Falmouth.

Barge crews after a celebration at the rear of the Commercial Inn

The regattas were fine occasions. The best lug-and-mizzen boat was the "Daisy Belle". Another was the "Pride of the Hills". Boats came from other villages to compete. Places like Coombe. There was a board at Vivian's Quay and when the tide reached it we knew that there was 12ft.6ins. of water.

When work was slack men would go oyster-dredging. A licence for one dredge was 12/6d. We got paid 2/6d. for every 1,000 oysters. The silt coming down from the mines wasn't good for the oyster beds in Carrick Roads. Fred Bryant built me my first dredging boat in 1921. Another Bryant, Jack, was a tin assayer.

The beech woods opposite Devoran owned by the Tremaynes had pheasants in them and sometimes they would be poached by men with boats. Once the railway closed the village was very poor and quiet. There was a horse bus run by Mr. George Dungey of Carclew Terrace. It was painted bright green and had the word "Express" in white. It could carry six passengers inside (if they weren't all large!). The older ladies sat inside whilst younger folk and boys sat outside on the roof seat - until they came to a hill when they would have to walk up. A "drug", a metal wedge, was used to drag along as a brake when going downhill. Two horses were used. The bus drove from Devoran to Truro on Mondays and Wednesdays whilst on Fridays it went to Redruth. Mr. Dungey had one-horse cabs as well as the bus.

You couldn't work far away until the motor bus came in 1922. Visicks were always operating as long as I can remember and the foundry at Perranarworthal was in use as a mill. Barges brought up loads of 200 sacks of grain from Falmouth, lowering their masts to get under the bridge by the "Norway".

Barge moored in the Perran River

A little shop on the Quay by the engine house was run by Billy Bray who made leather seaboots for the sailors whilst another cobbler was Jimmy Skewes at the bottom of Market Street.

Bands were both a strong interest and source of entertainment before the radio. I was in Perranwell Band at first but we were able to start the "Bleak House Band", based at that house when Feock Band broke up and we purchased some of their instruments. There was myself and up to ten others and we carried on until 1929.

Miss L. Webber - born 1907

I was born at Narabo Vale. My father, Edward Webber, served in the locomotive department of the railway and was a driver-in-charge at the age of 18. During the First World War, while he was under call-up age, he did voluntary ambulance work at St. Clement Naval Hospital (though he wouldn't wear his red cross armband in Truro because he was a St. John's man!). He drove the last train in Devoran in 1915, having nursed "Miner" carefully during her last years. The call-up age kept coming down and when it reached him, instead of going in the Forces, he was sent to Yorkshire to drive a train at the Rotherham Ironworks. Before the War I remember my Uncle Walter going down to operate the "Sluice."

The Bleak House Band
Back row: Wm. (farmer) Trebilcock, Will Trebilcock, Gordon Marshall, Reg Michell, - - - ,
Front row: Dick and Charlie Trebilcock on either side of Frank Marshall and Jackie Marshall

We had a "Hospital Sunday" once a year, organised by the Robartes Lodge of Oddfellows whose meetings were held upstairs at the Market House (you needed the password to get in!). There would be a parade round the village led by Carharrack Band and donations collected. A short service at St. John's or the Methodist Church (alternate years) was followed by a concert on the "field". The amount of money collected and handed to Royal Cornwall Infirmary would determine the number of "recommends" that the Lodge could make that year on behalf of poor people from Devoran who needed treatment.

There were some refugee children in Devoran in the 1914-18 War. They had strong foreign accents and, as Catholics, went to Church in Truro which meant walking both ways.

I enjoyed Devoran School. Mr. Cock, the headmaster, was very conscientious; at week-ends he would mend windows and other jobs rather than wait for the Council to come. He would give extra tuition to children wanting to sit scholarships and they would come to school an hour early for this.

My first job was to "do time" as a trainee shop assistant at the high class drapery store of N. Gill & Sons in Truro. For the first two years there was no pay at all, then 2/- a week until you thought you could go to Major Gill and justify asking more.

Some staff lived on the premises and there was a matron and a cook for them.My only bus from Devoran got in about 9.00 am so I suffered remarks about "doing Bank hours" but I didn't get home till late, sometimes walking over the "flats" from Perranwell Station to Carnon Gate where I then lived. Stocktaking was a very busy time. Each department made out its lists and when they were checked, you were fined 1d. for any errors in arithmetic. I remember how, every year, a lady from one of the big mansions would quietly go round choosing Christmas presents for all her staff.

I remember the Tea Treats at Devoran House, with saffron buns and sugary tea. We enjoyed trips in horse-drawn carriages and buses - but sometimes the passengers had to get out and walk up the hills to save the horse! There were many shops in Devoran. We liked the biscuits sold by Mary Michell at the bottom of Commercial Hill. She had a big turnover so they were fresher and you got a lovely selection for 6d. from her glass-topped tins.

Devoran Church Tea - 1919

Mrs. Tremayne at Carclew had the first motor car here - the wheels jumped about on the bumpy roads and you had to stand close to the hedge for safety! One man in the village had a large red nose and some boys would ask him the time just to be able to stare at his nose! The Policeman was P.C. Kellow.

A Captain Kemp lived near the Commercial Inn and his two sons did very well, one becoming a Captain and the other a Commodore. Another Inn in Devoran was the "Robartes Arms", run by a Mrs. Gilbert who was very strict with her customers. They had to put a coin in a box if they used swear words and the money went to Royal Cornwall Infirmary.

Dick Ferris, born 1903.

My grandfather was "Foreman" Ferris, who was well known for the design and workmanship of the ships he built at "Yard". Stephens took over the business later. My father ran the "Crown & Anchor" in Devoran after we moved up from Feock when I was quite small. I remember getting wax tails for our kites from Billy Bray's shop. I attended Devoran School until we moved to Restronguet for father to take over the "Pandora Inn". When I was only 11 years old I was rowing the ferry across the creek - fare was 1d. each way.

I can remember the trains working at Devoran and Captain Michell, the pilot, putting lamps out in the creek to bring ships in at night. There were no trees along the edge of the Tram Road like today. A man named Martin looked after the three horses; one was named "Madam". They were very obedient. The spare engine, "Spitfire" was painted red and we called her "The Red Lion".

The doctor at Devoran was a Dr. Edwards. I remember a boy drowning near the sluice pond. He had dived in headfirst and got stuck in the mud. The whole village was in mourning.

There was a market in Lemon Street in what's now the Church Hall. We kept pigs behind the "Crown & Anchor" and there was a butcher Phillips at Lower Quay. Pengillys' grain stores were at the bottom of Lemon Street.

Captain Tremayne had a yacht called "Jason". I used to go aboard a three masted schooner called "Mary Celine" where the Captain, named Pooley, would usually give us tea. There were many ships laid up in the Fal after the First War and I worked on them, cleaning and repairing. They had mostly been bought by Greeks. Then I worked on yachts in the summer and went oyster-dredging in the winter. I was on a steam yacht called "Grenade", sailing out of Southampton. I joined the sailing barge "May Blossom", 75 tons, bringing stone to several places near here; Tresillian, Point, Devoran and Perran Wharf. There were some steam barges too.

I remember the tall chimney stack at Point being used to build houses there; brick instead of the usual stone.

During the 1939-45 War our barge worked for the Americans, taking stone to Tolverne. The "Mary" barge had been built in Devoran. I worked later in pipe-laying, taking water to Tregony, Place and Portscatho on the Roseland. When the pumping-house was built in Greenbank Road it was difficult to find a bottom for the foundations, the concrete just kept disappearing!

AN EVENING CRUISE

To approach Devoran by sea today, on a rising tide, is a wholly pleasurable experience. There may be a few remnants of industry but these would have to be pointed out to a visitor. On entering Restronguet Creek the first temptation would be to tie up alongside the pontoon of the "Pandora Inn", a charming thatched inn which caters for locals and for visiting yachtsmen alike - with hot showers available for the latter!. Its catering has a fine reputation and the low, beamed ceilings and nooks and crannies are no modern sham. They have borne witness to a wealth of history since the 13th. century. Originally the "Passage House Inn", its second name was the "Ship Inn" but even this was changed in the 1790s when Captain Edward Edwards became the landlord. He had commanded H.M.S. "Pandora" when the ship was sent to hunt down mutineers from H.M.S. "Bounty" but had the misfortune to lose his ship on the return journey. He was held responsible and dismissed from the Navy.

Continuing up creek, and taking care to avoid the "spit" of sand near the south west shore by the old coal yard quay, we would pass on the right the sheltered side of the narrow Restronguet Point leading into Harcourt whilst to the left would be seen the woods and farmland of Crownick. Ahead, the huge artificial island formed for the 1835 mining venture, marked by a few stakes around and a cairn of stones at the centre, would require attention. Steering to starboard to enter Penpol Creek (modern spelling - old Cornish called for 2 Ls) would lead to where a boatyard thrived until recently, whilst at the head of navigation there used to be a bonemill, its pond no longer enclosed, near the present stepping stones.

Regaining the main creek we pass Point Quay. This quay has just become a public amenity area managed by the Point Quay Association and is the home of one of the most popular of the Fal Regattas. Together with a line of adjoining quays, it saw industrial trade on a large scale (and prior to Devoran's as it has deeper water) including the smelting of lead, tin and zinc. It was then called Daniells' Point, after one of the early entrepreneurs, and adjacent to it was Lemon Quay. Point was the terminus for the horse-drawn railway from Devoran and, in recent scrub clearance, an old lime kiln has been revealed.

On, up the creek, past the farms of Halwyn and Tregunwith and the wooded headland of Carsawsan on the left, opposite the beach inlet of Chycoose, one approaches the seaward end of the old streamworks. Nothing of them to be seen at high water except the gaunt remains of the Carnon Stream Mine on the right, just before the wide opening of Tallacks Creek, but at half tide the first part of the bank protecting the Perran River would be visible.

If this channel was taken, it would lead past the former Lemon, later Tremayne, lands of Carclew, the remains of their quay still existing, past little islands which gradually give way to a permanent embankment. A left turn up Perran Creek and, if your craft is tiny, the chance to pass the "Norway Inn" on your way up to Perran Foundry. The inn was so named because of the Norwegian timber ships which once berthed near there with cargoes for the mines but today you would need a machete to hack your way through to that spot. There are plans to restore many of the old foundry buildings, forming a heritage centre and museum as well as residential accommodation.

On your return journey, if the tide still served, you could turn hard-a-port just before Carclew Quay and follow the narrow but deep channel of the Trewedna Stream under the main road to pass the old Visick engineering works. To reach Devoran means re-tracing steps, or rather ripples!, to the largest of the islands where a narrow cut gives access to the main creek and, approaching the village, you could secure alongside the newly-restored Devoran Quay (the original Narabo Quay) and visit the "Old Quay Inn", assuming you still have a thirst after your earlier stop!

The effort involved in purchasing and improving this, the seaward end of the old docks, becomes so obviously worthwhile as, from this point, one can see how the waterfront has become denied to the public. The residential building along Quay Road, followed by the industrial premises in Greenbank Road, has left very few points of access. Yes! Devoran still has some industry. A water-related one is the designing and building premises of the world-famous Wharram catamarans. Close by is the Devoran Window Company whilst, above the bridge to the left of the creek, the former Visick works are still used for engineering.

It would be hard to believe that the channels followed on this "trip" were once called the "gutter of the mining district"! Fortunately the mud has recovered to an extent from the injuries of a century ago and, at the lower end of the food chain, the worms have adapted to the arsenical substances (creating a place for themselves in biological textbooks) and the many varieties of wading birds seem to accept them well enough. The most common are the various gulls, herons, curlews, whimbrel, black tailed godwits, oystercatchers, greenshank, redshank, dunlin and sandpipers. In spring the shellduck (Britain's largest duck) are common whilst in autumn teal (the smallest) pay a visit. You may be lucky enough to catch the flash of a kingfisher in the Perran River or even the brilliant whiteness of a little egret. High above the southern shores a pair of buzzards frequently glide effortlessly among the thermals and of course a large range of country/garden birds inhabit the area. In the creek itself are eels, mullet and bass and occasionally a seal will come up from Carrick Roads and indulge in that well-known seal hobby of "watching humans watching them"!

The remains of the embankments are covered with thrift in May and June and, as this is a flower that enjoys metallic deposits, it has every opportunity to prosper here! The Perran Creek has silted up so much that it is largely water meadow but there is some salt marsh which is comparatively scarce in Cornwall. In summer the sea asters take over from the thrift but on the areas of mud that are on the edge of tidal covering there is a vigorous growth of samphire or glasswort. The shoreline sports such plants as feverfew, sea spurry and wild spinach. On the Carclew shore opposite Devoran is a large reed bed. Several old photographs taken from Devoran looking down the creek show the distinctive curve of oak trees at the Carsawsan bend and this seems quite unchanged today.

Childrens raft races are popular now

One of the many pleasing aspects of today is the extensive use made of their creek by the people of Devoran. In summer months all manner of small craft appear. The moored cruisers, the traditional rowing punts that leave the beach with fishermen trying their luck, perhaps making for the "Pandora" or just taking granny for an evening row. Windsurfers are a recent but dedicated body and swimming from the "island" has probably been popular for decades. Occasionally a "gig" will be seen and the Devoran Gig Club hope soon to become proud owners of one of these evocative craft. Racing skiffs appear from time to time, as do rubber dinghies and even experimental rafts built by children in preparation for the regatta or other events. Sailing dinghies abound and younger residents are fortunate in that the present Vicar, a keen sailor himself, founded the St. Petroc's Boat Club which offers the chance to "have a go", receive tuition and which, for many, will be the gateway to a nautical passion that will last all their lives.

As I write, the former Market Hall which was donated by Lord Robartes and subsequently became the Church Hall, is being incorporated into an extension of the school and Devoran Church has a fund-raising effort in progress to construct a new Parish Centre to replace it.

The village now is designated a "Conservation Area" and is in an "Area of Outstanding Natural Beauty". Close by are areas of "Great Scientific Value", "Great Landscape Value" and "Cornwall Nature Conservation Sites". Devoran has revived indeed but its colourful history is a part of it and, although few people can now remember the industrial past, there are many who are determined to preserve the memories of it for it these that make it
A DIFFERENT CORNISH VILLAGE.